MATCH OF THE DAY **ANNUAL 2021**

Colour your shirt in

Your surname

Shirt number

This book belongs to	Age
My favourite team is	
My favourite player is	
My highlight of 2020 was	

WELCOME!

You can also catch up with MOTD on BBC iPlayer!

Don't forget to keep watching MOTD, readers!

CHEERS, 2020!

What a year, huh? The past 12 months have had some unexpected twists and turns, nail-biting drama and awesome big-game moments. Here, we celebrate them all – and look forward to 2021. Get stuck in!

BBC One Don't miss *Match of the Day*, Saturdays and Sundays on BBC One and BBC Two!

UNSTOPPABLE Bayern Munich became European champs for the sixth time!

WHAT'S INSIDE YOUR MOTD ANNUAL?

p25 MOTD mag's interview zone!

p32 The ultimate celebration guide!

p40 FaceTime funnies!

MPIONS LEAGUE 2019/20

96 PAGES OF FOOTY FUN!

p44 The greatest ever pics of the GOAT!

p54 Epic A-Z of women's footy!

p82 FIFA FUT player histories!

PLUS 16 Amazing posters!

KYLIAN MBAPPE
FRANCE

MATCH of the DAY magazine

MBAPPÉ

96 PAC	90 DRI
84 SHO	39 DEF
78 PAS	75 PHY

BIG FAT TOP 10 SPECIAL!

Shot-stopping cats? Mega-money transfers? FIFA's fastest ballers? Yep, our 12-page guide of ledge lists has it all. Get stuck in, readers!

TURN OVER FOR MORE!

TOP 10 PREMIER LE

Here are English footy's net-busting kings of the top tier

10

149 GOALS / 351 APPS
LES FERDINAND

9

150 GOALS / 326 APPS
MICHAEL OWEN

8

162 GOALS / 496 APPS
JERMAIN DEFOE

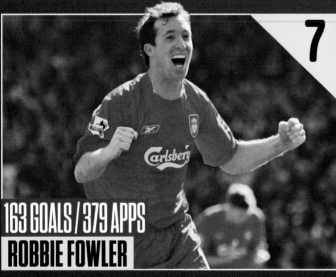

7

163 GOALS / 379 APPS
ROBBIE FOWLER

6

175 GOALS / 258 APPS
THIERRY HENRY

5

177 GOALS / 609 APPS
FRANK LAMPARD

TOP 10 PREMIER LEAGUE CLEAN SHEETS!

10 PETER SCHMEICHEL
128 CLEAN SHEETS / 310 APPS

=7 BRAD FRIEDEL
132 CLEAN SHEETS / 450 APPS

=7 TIM HOWARD
132 CLEAN SHEETS / 399 APPS

=7 EDWIN VAN DER SAR
132 CLEAN SHEETS / 313 APPS

AGUE GOALSCORERS!

180 GOALS / 263 APPS
SERGIO AGUERO
4

187 GOALS / 414 APPS
ANDY COLE
3

208 GOALS / 491 APPS
WAYNE ROONEY
2

260 GOALS / 441 APPS
ALAN SHEARER
1

6 PEPE REINA
134 CLEAN SHEETS / 291 APPS

5 NIGEL MARTYN
137 CLEAN SHEETS / 372 APPS

4 DAVID SEAMAN
140 CLEAN SHEETS / 344 APPS

3 MARK SCHWARZER
151 CLEAN SHEETS / 514 APPS

2 DAVID JAMES
169 CLEAN SHEETS / 572 APPS

1 PETR CECH
202 CLEAN SHEETS / 443 APPS

TOP 10 BIGGEST TRANSFERS EVER!

1

£200m
NEYMAR
BARCELONA TO PSG – AUG 2017

2

£165.7m
KYLIAN MBAPPE
MONACO TO PSG – AUG 2017

3

£150m
EDEN HAZARD
CHELSEA TO REAL MADRID – JUN 2019

4

£142m
PHILIPPE COUTINHO
LIVERPOOL TO BARCELONA – JAN 2018

5

£135.5m
OUSMANE DEMBELE
BORUSSIA DORTMUND TO BARCELONA – AUG 2017

6

£133m
JOAO FELIX
BENFICA TO ATLETICO MADRID – JUL 2019

7

£107m
ANTOINE GRIEZMANN
ATLETICO MADRID TO BARCELONA – JUL 2019

8

£99.2m
CRISTIANO RONALDO
REAL MADRID TO JUVENTUS – JUL 2018

9

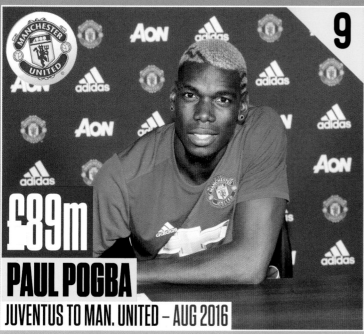

£89m
PAUL POGBA
JUVENTUS TO MAN. UNITED – AUG 2016

10

£86m
GARETH BALE
TOTTENHAM TO REAL MADRID – SEP 2013

All stats correct up to 6 July 2020

TOP 10 FASTEST FIFA 20 PLAYERS

1
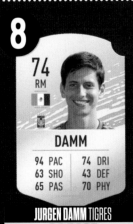
74 RW
ADAMA TRAORÉ

96	PAC	83	DRI
60	SHO	31	DEF
61	PAS	75	PHY

ADAMA TRAORE WOLVES
96 PACE

2

89 ST
MBAPPÉ

96	PAC	90	DRI
84	SHO	39	DEF
78	PAS	75	PHY

KYLIAN MBAPPE PSG
96 PACE

3
86 LW
SANÉ

95	PAC	86	DRI
81	SHO	38	DEF
79	PAS	70	PHY

LEROY SANE MAN. CITY
95 PACE

4
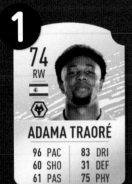
66 LB
CHALÁ

95	PAC	57	DRI
46	SHO	63	DEF
54	PAS	65	PHY

ANIBAL CHALA TOLUCA
95 PACE

5
69 ST
NAGAI

95	PAC	67	DRI
64	SHO	41	DEF
60	PAS	74	PHY

KENSUKE NAGAI FC TOKYO
95 PACE

6

82 RM
GELSON MARTINS

95	PAC	86	DRI
71	SHO	47	DEF
74	PAS	61	PHY

GELSON MARTINS MONACO
95 PACE

7

88 ST
AUBAMEYANG

94	PAC	80	DRI
85	SHO	37	DEF
75	PAS	69	PHY

P.E AUBAMEYANG ARSENAL
94 PACE

8
74 RM
DAMM

94	PAC	74	DRI
63	SHO	43	DEF
65	PAS	70	PHY

JURGEN DAMM TIGRES
94 PACE

9
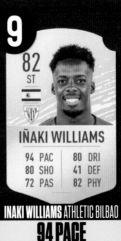
82 ST
IÑAKI WILLIAMS

94	PAC	80	DRI
80	SHO	41	DEF
72	PAS	82	PHY

INAKI WILLIAMS ATHLETIC BILBAO
94 PACE

10

71 RM
KIM IN SEONG

94	PAC	72	DRI
60	SHO	32	DEF
64	PAS	49	PHY

KIM IN SEONG ULSAN HYUNDAI
94 PACE

TOP 10 PICS OF ANIMALS PLAYING FOOTY!

Footy is for everyone – top-bins-saving cats, ball-bursting elephants and, er, hamsters

10
PIG CONTROL!

9
POLAR PASS!

8
FISH TACKLE!

7
MONKEY THROW-IN!

6
TIGER DRIBBLE!

HAMSTER CATCH!

4

SEA LION SKILLS!

3

5
ELEPHANT TOUCH!

2
DOG HEADER!

CAT SAVE!

1

TOP 10 CHAMPIONS OF WORLD FOOTBALL!

Which clubs have won the most domestic league titles?

ENGLAND

1	MAN. UNITED	20
2	LIVERPOOL	19
3	ARSENAL	13
4	EVERTON	9
5	ASTON VILLA	7
6	SUNDERLAND	6
=	CHELSEA	6
=	MAN. CITY	6
9	NEWCASTLE	4
=	SHEFFIELD WEDNESDAY	4
10	WOLVES	3
=	LEEDS	3
=	HUDDERSFIELD	3
=	BLACKBURN	3

SCOTLAND

1	RANGERS	54
2	CELTIC	51
3	ABERDEEN	4
=	HEARTS	4
=	HIBERNIAN	4
6	DUMBARTON	2
7	MOTHERWELL	1
=	KILMARNOCK	1
=	DUNDEE	1
=	DUNDEE UNITED	1
=	THIRD LANARK	1
8-10	NO-ONE!	

GERMANY

1	BAYERN MUNICH	30
2	NURNBERG	9
3	BORUSSIA DORTMUND	8
4	SCHALKE	7
5	HAMBURG	6
6	STUTTGART	5
7	B. MONCHENGLADBACH	4
=	WERDER BREMEN	4
=	KAISERSLAUTERN	4
10	COLOGNE	3
=	LOKOMITOV LEIPZIG	3
=	GREUTHER FURTH	3

FRANCE

1	MARSEILLE	10
=	SAINT-ETIENNE	10
3	PSG	9
4	MONACO	8
=	NANTES	8
6	LYON	7
7	BORDEAUX	6
=	REIMS	6
=	ROUBAIX	6
10	LILLE	5

ITALY

1	JUVENTUS	36
2	AC MILAN	18
=	INTER MILAN	18
4	GENOA	9
5	TORINO	7
=	BOLOGNA	7
=	PRO VERCELLI	7
8	ROMA	3
9	LAZIO	2
=	NAPOLI	2
=	FIORENTINA	2
10	SAMPDORIA	1
=	HELLAS VERONA	1
=	CAGLIARI	1
=	NOVESE	1

SPAIN

1	REAL MADRID	33
2	BARCELONA	26
3	ATLETICO MADRID	10
4	ATHLETIC BILBAO	8
5	VALENCIA	6
6	REAL SOCIEDAD	2
7	DEPORTIVO LA CORUNA	1
=	SEVILLA	1
=	REAL BETIS	1
10	NO-ONE!	

All stats correct up to 28 August 2020

TOP 10 INTERNATIONAL MEN'S FOOTY SPECIAL!

Goals, caps and World Cup wins – your go-to guide to international football

MOST GOALS IN A MEN'S WORLD CUP!

	PLAYER		GOALS	GAMES
1	MIROSLAV KLOSE	GERMANY	16	24
2	RONALDO	BRAZIL	15	19
3	GERD MULLER	GERMANY	14	13
4	JUST FONTAINE	FRANCE	13	6
5	PELE	BRAZIL	12	14
6	SANDOR KOCSIS	HUNGARY	11	5
7	JURGEN KLINSMANN	GERMANY	11	17
8	HELMUT RAHN	GERMANY	10	10
9	GARY LINEKER	ENGLAND	10	12
=	GABRIEL BATISTUTA	ARGENTINA	10	12
10	TEOFILO CUBILLAS	PERU	10	13

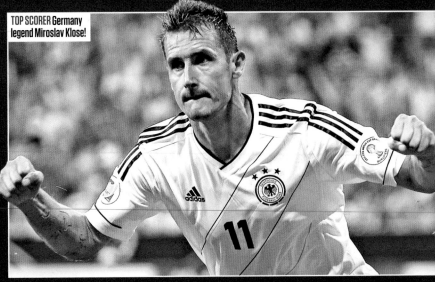

TOP SCORER Germany legend Miroslav Klose!

CUP FOR IT Brazil have claimed a record five World Cup wins!

MOST TROPHY WINS IN A MEN'S WORLD CUP!

	COUNTRY	TROPHIES	APPS
1	BRAZIL	5	21
2	GERMANY	4	19
3	ITALY	4	18
4	ARGENTINA	2	17
5	FRANCE	2	15
6	ENGLAND	1	15
7	SPAIN*	1	15
8	URUGUAY**	1	15
9-10	ONLY EIGHT WC WINNERS!		

*Spain are seventh due to overall points gained
** Uruguay are eighth due to games played and overall po

TOP 10 BOOTS OF ALL TIME!

Tick your fave ever pair of boots from our list

1 NIKE TIEMPO   2 ADIDAS COPA MUNDIAL   3 NIKE CTR360 MAESTRI   4 ADIDAS F50

MOST GOALS SCORED FOR ENGLAND!

	PLAYER	GOALS	GAMES
1	WAYNE ROONEY	53	120
2	BOBBY CHARLTON	49	106
3	GARY LINEKER	48	80
4	JIMMY GREAVES	44	57
5	MICHAEL OWEN	40	89
6	HARRY KANE	32	45
7	NAT LOFTHOUSE	30	33
8	ALAN SHEARER	30	63
9	TOM FINNEY	30	76
10	VIVIAN WOODWARD	29	23

ROO BEAUTY Wazza is England's all-time leading goalscorer!

MOST INTERNATIONAL GOALS!

	PLAYER	COUNTRY	GOALS	GAMES
1	ALI DAEI	IRAN	109	149
2	CRISTIANO RONALDO	PORTUGAL	99	164
3	MOKHTAR DAHARI	MALAYSIA	85	140
4	FERENC PUSKAS	HUNGARY	84	85
5	KUNISHIGE KAMAMOTO	JAPAN	80	84
6	GODFREY CHITALU	ZAMBIA	79	111
7	HUSSEIN SAEED	IRAQ	78	137
8	PELE	BRAZIL	77	92
9	BASHAR ABDULLAH	KUWAIT	75	132
10	SUNIL CHHETRI	INDIA	72	115

GOAL KING Ali Daei of Iran has the most international goals!

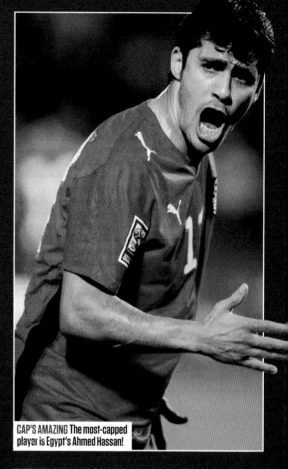

CAP'S AMAZING The most-capped player is Egypt's Ahmed Hassan!

MOST INTERNATIONAL CAPS!

	PLAYER	COUNTRY	CAPS
1	AHMED HASSAN	EGYPT	184
2	MOHAMED AL-DEAYEA	SAUDI ARABIA	178
3	CLAUDIO SUAREZ	MEXICO	177
4	GIANLUIGI BUFFON	ITALY	176
5	AHMED MUBARAK	OMAN	175
=	BADER AL-MUTAWA	KUWAIT	175
6	HOSSAM HASSAN	EGYPT	170
=	SERGIO RAMOS	SPAIN	170
7	IVAN HURTADO	ECUADOR	168
8	VITALIJS ASTAFJEVS	EGYPT	167
=	IKER CASILLAS	SPAIN	167
9	COBI JONES	USA	164
=	CRISTIANO RONALDO	PORTUGAL	164
10	MOHAMMED AL-KHILAIWI	SAUDI ARABIA	163
=	MAYNOR FIGUEROA	HONDURAS	163

5 MIZUNO WAVE CUP   6 NIKE AIR ZOOM TOTAL 90   7 UMBRO SPECIALI   8 PUMA KING   9 NIKE MERCURIAL VAPOR   10 ADIDAS PREDATOR

TOP 10 WOMEN'S FOOTY SPECIAL!

From the World Cup to the WSL, five fire lists to level up your knowledge

BRAZILIANT Top scorer Marta!

MOST GOALS IN A WOMEN'S WORLD CUP!

	PLAYER	COUNTRY	GOALS	GAMES
1	MARTA	BRAZIL	17	20
2	BIRGIT PRINZ	GERMANY	14	24
3	ABBY WAMBACH	USA	14	25
4	MICHELLE AKERS	USA	12	13
5	SUN WREN	CHINA	11	20
6	CRISTIANE	BRAZIL	11	21
7	BETTINA WIEGMANN	GERMANY	11	22
8	ANN KRISTIN AARONES	NORWAY	10	11
9	HEIDI MOHR	GERMANY	10	12
10	CHRISTINE SINCLAIR	USA	10	21

MOST CAPS FOR THE LIONESSES!

	PLAYER	GAMES
1	FARA WILLIAMS	172
2	JILL SCOTT	149
3	KAREN CARNEY	144
4	ALEX SCOTT	140
5	CASEY STONEY	130
6	STEPH HOUGHTON	120
7	GILLIAN COULTARD	119
8	KELLY SMITH	114
9	RACHEL UNITT	102
=	ENI ALUKO	102
10	ELLEN WHITE	92

FAB FARA England ledge Fara Williams!

TOP 10 UCL GOALSCORERS EVER! The sickest strikers Europe has seen

10 ZLATAN IBRAHIMOVIC
48 GOALS / 120 APPS

9 ANDRIY SHEVCHENKO
48 GOALS / 100 APPS

8 ALFREDO DI STEFANO
49 GOALS / 58 APPS

7 THIERRY HENRY
50 GOALS / 112 APPS

NICK NIK Parris has bagged the most WSL goals ever!

MOST TOP-FLIGHT LEAGUE TITLES!

	CLUB	TITLES
1	ARSENAL	15
2	CHELSEA	3
=	CHARLTON	3
3	LIVERPOOL	2
=	DONACASTER BELLES	2
=	SUNDERLAND	2
4	MAN. CITY	1
=	EVERTON	1
=	FULHAM	1
5-10	The title has only ever been won by the teams above	

GUNNER GLEE Arsenal have won a record 15 league titles!

MOST EUROPEAN TITLES!

	CLUB	TITLES
1	LYON	6
2	FRANKFURT	4
3	UMEA	2
=	TURBINE POTSDAM	2
=	WOLFSBURG	2
4	ARSENAL	1
=	DUISBURG	1
5-10	The title has only ever been won by the teams above	

LYON QUEENS Lyon have won a record six UCL titles!

MOST GOALS IN WSL HISTORY!

	PLAYER	GOALS
1	NIKITA PARRIS	49
2	ELLEN WHITE	47
3	JORDAN NOBBS	43
4	VIVIANNE MIEDEMA	42
5	BETHANY ENGLAND	41
6	FARA WILLIAMS	40
7	KIM LITTLE	39
8	BETH MEAD	37
9	RACHEL WILLIAMS	37
	TONI DUGGAN	36
	ENI ALUKO	36
10	JI SO-YUN	35

RUUD VAN NISTELROOY
56 GOALS / 73 APPS

5 KARIM BENZEMA
65 GOALS / 120 APPS

4 ROBERT LEWANDOWSKI
68 GOALS / 90 APPS

3 RAUL
71 GOALS / 142 APPS

2 LIONEL MESSI
115 GOALS / 143 APPS

1 CRISTIANO RONALDO
130 GOALS / 170 APPS

Catch up with The Women's Football Show on BBC iPlayer

All stats correct up to 28 August 2020

TRUE OR FALSE?

You've simply got to decide if these statements are fact or fiction

1

NORTH KOREAN leader Kim Jong-Un won two caps for his country in 2003 – he even scored in an Asian Cup match against Myanmar!

TRUE: ☑ FALSE: ☑

2

LEAGUE TWO team Crawley Town were originally called Creepy Crawley FC because they were founded by a group of insect enthusiasts. The club dropped the Creepy part of its name in 1979!

TRUE: ☑ FALSE: ☑

3

STRIKER TEEMU PUKKI was raised by a herd of reindeer in a forest in northern Finland, after running away from home when he was five years old!

TRUE: ☑ FALSE: ☑

4

ACCORDING TO Man. United's official club doctors, Harry Maguire's head weighs the same as four fully grown North American beavers!

TRUE: ☑ FALSE: ☑

5

Other crisps are available!

LEICESTER STRIKER Jamie Vardy eats nothing but roast beef Monster Munch for his breakfast, lunch and dinner – and has done since he was 12!

TRUE: ☑ FALSE: ☑

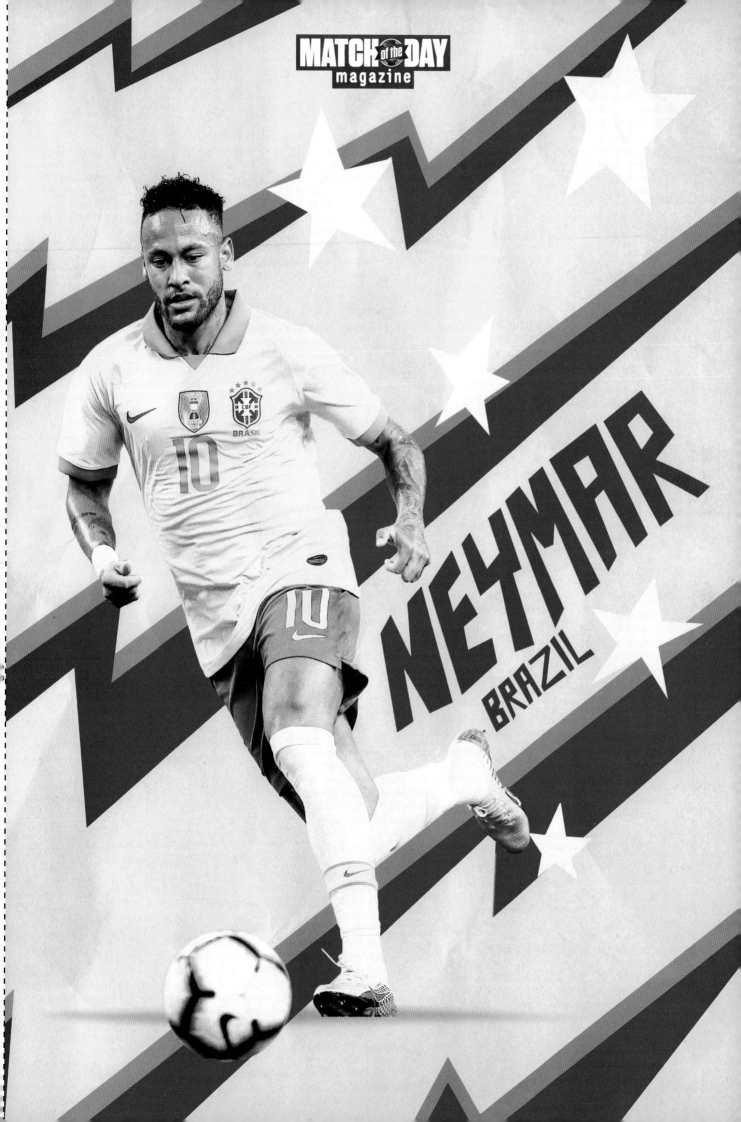

CAPTION THIS LOLS!

Pull on your funny fez and write a LOL for these pics

OUR CAPTION: I could make a worldie assist with my eyes closed!

YOUR CAPTION

OUR CAPTION: Virgil, there's a MASSIVE spider on yer shorts!

YOUR CAPTION

OUR CAPTION: Shelvey wet his pants – pass it on!

YOUR CAPTION

OUR CAPTION: Here's the emergency hair wax you asked for!

YOUR CAPTION

I'll caption you in a minute, Ketch!

You couldn't even caption a cold, Paz!

OUR CAPTION: Is this snakes and ladders, Trent?

YOUR CAPTION

OUR CAPTION: Giant dartboard invades pitch!

YOUR CAPTION

OUR CAPTION: My secret? I must be at one with the net!

YOUR CAPTION

WANT MORE CAPTIONS?
Visit MOTDmag.com/caption-this to view our caption gallery and submit LOLs of your own!

TURN OVER FOR MORE!

ENTER MOTD MAG'S

INTERVIEW ZONE!

Five footy megastars. Four awesome chats. All in one place

INTERVIEW 1

KEVIN DE BRUYNE

MANCHESTER CITY
18 94

Man. City's assist king talks about his boyhood team, winding up pals and his big footy dreams!

Yes Kev! Who did you support as a kid?

DE BRUYNE SAYS: "I was a Liverpool fan. My family that live in England were all Liverpool supporters so I was, too. I loved Michael Owen because I was really small like him and quick, too!"

OWEN GOALS
Kev loved Mo!

Best advice you had as a kid?

DE BRUYNE SAYS: "To enjoy football and have fun! These days kids get a lot of pressure, but the most important thing is to enjoy playing football. If you don't it's better to look for something else to do!"

Best FIFA player you've ever faced?

DE BRUYNE SAYS: "At City, I think Raheem is very good. If you lose against me then you're pretty bad. I Just play friendly games, really. I like playing with my mates because we wind each other up!"

What's your fave ever goal?

DE BRUYNE SAYS: "Against the USA in the 2014 World Cup and Brazil in 2018. My first goal was also very important to me. It was headed to me on the edge of the box and I took it on the bounce – it hit the post and went in. It was a derby, so that was pretty nice!"

WHAT A HIT De Bruyne nets against Brazil!

De Bruyne made his debut for Belgium against Turkey in 2010!

MAG-NIFICENT Kev with his MOTD mag!

" **I loved Michael Owen, because I was really small like him and quick, too!**"

DE BRUYNE

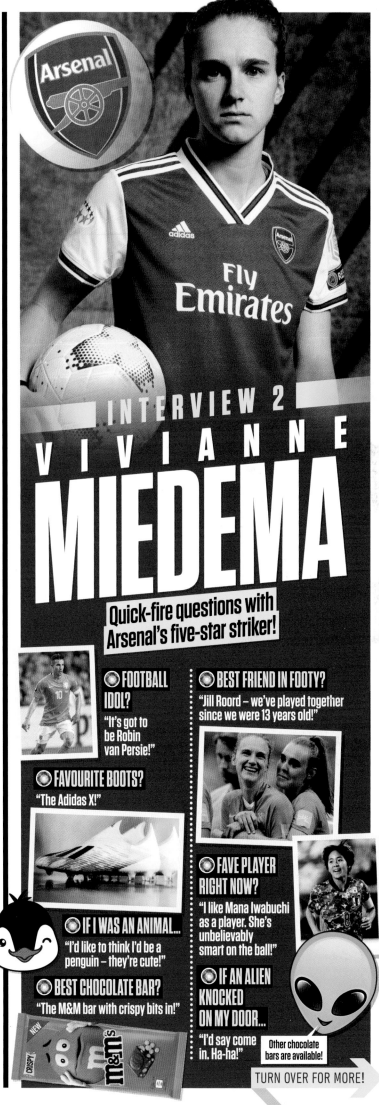

INTERVIEW 2

VIVIANNE MIEDEMA

Quick-fire questions with Arsenal's five-star striker!

FOOTBALL IDOL?
"It's got to be Robin van Persie!"

FAVOURITE BOOTS?
"The Adidas X!"

IF I WAS AN ANIMAL...
"I'd like to think I'd be a penguin – they're cute!"

BEST CHOCOLATE BAR?
"The M&M bar with crispy bits in!"

BEST FRIEND IN FOOTY?
"Jill Roord – we've played together since we were 13 years old!"

FAVE PLAYER RIGHT NOW?
"I like Mana Iwabuchi as a player. She's unbelievably smart on the ball!"

IF AN ALIEN KNOCKED ON MY DOOR...
"I'd say come in. Ha-ha!"

Other chocolate bars are available!

TURN OVER FOR MORE!

INTERVIEW 3
THE F2

Billy & Jez bring the banter and talk new footy rules, their ultimate baller and fave ever F2 moment!

BILLY!

What's your best moment as The F2?

JEZ SAYS: "Performing at the Ballon d'Or award show – that's when we realised we had something special. We basically stole the show and got a great ovation from the most important people in world football!"

GOLDEN BOYS Billy & Jez at the Ballon d'Or award show!

Who is the ultimate footballer?

BILLY SAYS: "Virgil van Dijk. He's fast, reads the game well, scores goals, takes free-kicks, wins challenges – what's Van Dijk missing from his game? You know if you put him up front, he'd score as well. He'd make the runs and win every header!"

Which player you've filmed with surprised you the most?

JEZ SAYS: "Julian Draxler's footwork at PSG was unbelievable. We did this speed test with Draxler and I've never seen anyone dribble so quickly in and out of poles!"

Who would you say you both play like?

BILLY SAYS: "For Jez, I'd go Isco. His dribbling is unbelievable and that's what he's best at – either him or Eden Hazard!"

JEZ SAYS: "For Billy, I'd say Mbappe. They've both got pace, skill and score goals!"

What rule would you love to add to footy?

BILLY SAYS: "For ten minutes, your boss can choose at any point that their team's next goal counts for two goals. Or if the team gets a pen, the manager takes it!"

DRIBBLE KING Julian Draxler!

GREAT READ Friends of the mag Billy & Jez!

JEZ!

"We stole the show at the Ballon d'Or and got a great ovation!"

JEZ

Dybs was in the Serie A Team of the Year in 2015-16, 2016-17 and 2017-18!

FIRST DYBS Paulo tucks into his fave magazine!

INTERVIEW 4
PAULO
DYBALA

Argentina's awesome attacker chats to MOTD!

What Prem players do you like watching?

DYBALA SAYS: "Paul Pogba – because he is my friend and a great player, Kevin De Bruyne because he is skilful and Harry Kane because he scores in so many different ways. Also, Aubameyang – he is so fast!"

Which young Juventus player has a really big future in football?

DYBALA SAYS: "There are so many young players who can have a great career. At Juventus, I'd choose Rodrigo Bentancur!"

Who's the best baller you've played against in real life – and who's the best you've played with on FIFA?

DYBALA SAYS: "I'm lucky to have played with and against Lionel Messi and Cristiano Ronaldo – for sure, they are the best players the world has seen for many years. In *FIFA*? Maradona and Ronaldo. As a kid I loved Ronaldinho!"

What's your fave FIFA game mode?

DYBALA SAYS: "I like to play FUT or Champions League mode, however I really enjoy playing with my friends on No Rules and Survival modes!"

RONALDO

PORTUGAL

HuW bIG Is YuUr GKuUNU?

Arsenal

EMIRATES STADIUM
Capacity: 60,704

Aston Villa
VILLA PARK
Capacity: 42,785

Brighton
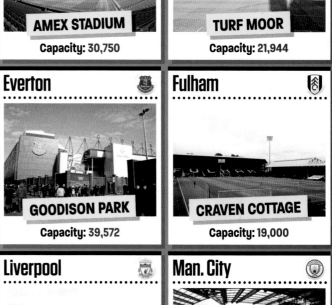
AMEX STADIUM
Capacity: 30,750

Burnley
TURF MOOR
Capacity: 21,944

Chelsea

STAMFORD BRIDGE
Capacity: 40,834

Crystal Palace

SELHURST PARK
Capacity: 25,486

Everton

GOODISON PARK
Capacity: 39,572

Fulham

CRAVEN COTTAGE
Capacity: 19,000

Leeds

ELLAND ROAD
Capacity: 37,890

Leicester

KING POWER STADIUM
Capacity: 32,243

Liverpool

ANFIELD
Capacity: 53,394

Man. City
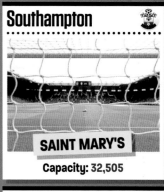
ETIHAD STADIUM
Capacity: 55,097

Man. United

OLD TRAFFORD
Capacity: 74,879

Newcastle

ST JAMES' PARK
Capacity: 52,388

Sheffield United

BRAMALL LANE
Capacity: 32,125

Southampton

SAINT MARY'S
Capacity: 32,505

Tottenham
TOTTENHAM HOTSPUR STADIUM
Capacity: 62,303

West Brom
THE HAWTHORNS
Capacity: 26,850

West Ham
LONDON STADIUM
Capacity: 60,000

Wolves
MOLINEUX
Capacity: 32,050

LET'S CE

EBRATE!

Boom! You've just scored a scorcher and now it's all eyes on you. The big question – how are you going to celebrate?

LUCKILY FOR YOU, WE'VE GOT AN ULTIMATE GUIDE TO FOOTBALL'S FAMOUS CELEBRATIONS!

TURN OVER FOR MORE!

THE KNEE SLIDE!

Do: Ensure the grass is damp, preferably wet

Don't: Injure yourself doing it on a bone-dry pitch

DIFFICULTY: ★★★☆☆   STYLE: ★★★★☆

THE POINT TO THE SKY!

Do: Copy what Lukaku and Messi do

Don't: Strain a finger – all kinds of lame

DIFFICULTY: ★☆☆☆☆
STYLE: ★★☆☆☆

THE SOMERSAULT!

Do: Leave this one to the professionals

Don't: Even think about trying this one at home

DIFFICULTY: ★★★★★   STYLE: ★★★★★

THE SALUTE!

Do: Give it the pomp and authority of a proper military procession

Don't: Whack yourself in the eyes and stumble into the crowd wailing

DIFFICULTY: ★☆☆☆☆
STYLE: ★★☆☆☆

ICONIC CELES!

Some superstar ballers even have their very own legendary celebrations – check out these classics

RONALDO

SHEARER

THE I CAN'T HEAR YOU!

Do: If you've been getting abuse from the opposition fans

Don't: If your team is still losing the match – it's not a good look

DIFFICULTY: ★★☆☆☆   STYLE: ★★★☆☆

THE BADGE KISS!

Do: This to become a fans' favourite

Don't: Do this against your old club

DIFFICULTY: ★★☆☆☆
STYLE: ★★★☆☆

THE THIS IS MY CLUB!

Do: Show you love your club

Don't: Point to the kit maker by mistake

DIFFICULTY: ★★☆☆☆
STYLE: ★★☆☆☆

THE CORNER FLAG ATTACK!

Do: Imagine the flag is your ninja nemesis and karate it good

Don't: Get hit in the wotsits by the rebounding flag – huge fail

DIFFICULTY: ★★★★☆   STYLE: ★★★★☆

MBAPPE

STURRIDGE

HAALAND

RONALDINHO

GRIEZMANN

TURN OVER FOR MORE!

THE RUN TO THE BENCH!

Do: This if you want to pay special thanks to one of the coaching staff

Don't: Run to the wrong dugout by mistake and hug the opposing team

DIFFICULTY: ★★☆☆☆

STYLE: ★★★☆☆

THE SHIRT OFF!

Do: If you've just bagged a last-minute winner

Don't: If you've already been shown a yellow card

DIFFICULTY: ★★☆☆☆ **STYLE:** ★★★☆☆

THE SHUSH!

Do: If you've been getting stick

Don't: Aim this one at the gaffer

DIFFICULTY: ★★☆☆☆

STYLE: ★★☆☆☆

THE ARMS OUT!

Do: This when you net a hat-trick

Don't: If your goal is a consolation

DIFFICULTY: ★☆☆☆☆

STYLE: ★★★☆☆

THE AIR PUNCH!

Do: Nail the landing or risk injury

Don't: Accidentally punch the ref

DIFFICULTY: ★★★☆☆

STYLE: ★★★☆☆

ICONIC CELES!

Some superstar ballers even have their very own legendary celebrations – check out these classics

BEBETO

CAVANI

THE THANK THE ASSISTER!

Do: Be humble and thank your mates

Don't: Point to the wrong team-mate

DIFFICULTY: ★☆☆☆☆

STYLE: ★☆☆☆☆

THE WHAT'S MY NAME!

Do: Turn your back to the crowd to show them who you are

Don't: Do this in front of the opposition supporters or players

DIFFICULTY: ★★★☆☆ **STYLE:** ★★★☆☆

THE KISS THE BOOT!

Do: Speak to a team-mate BEFORE the match so they know what to do

Don't: Step in dog poo during the game – disaster for your team-mate

DIFFICULTY: ★★★☆☆ **STYLE:** ★★★☆☆

THE RUSH TO THE CENTRE CIRCLE!

Do: If you're chasing a late equaliser or even a winner

Don't: Do this if you've just netted a last-minute winner

DIFFICULTY: ★★☆☆☆

STYLE: ★★☆☆☆

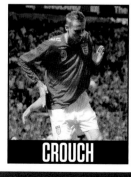  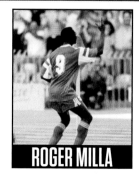  

CROUCH **LEWANDOWSKI** **ROGER MILLA** **OZIL** **RAPINOE**

MATCH of the DAY magazine

MESSI

ARGENTINA

MATCH of the DAY magazine

VAN DIJK #4

NETHERLANDS

FACETIME

Ever wondered what a superstar video call would be like?

WHEN C-RON KEEPS CALLING MESSI!

Peekaboo, Leo!

Knew I shouldn't have answered...

Woah, wrong number!

WHEN HARRY'S FINGER SLIPS!

Woof!

WHEN MOTD CALLS PEP FOR AN INTERVIEW!

Errrm, hello Pep!

Can you ring me back in five, Gaz?

FUNNIES!

I don't play FIFA. FIFA plays me.

Yeaaaaaah – okay, bro!

WHEN ZLATAN WANTS TO LINK FOR FIFA!

We'd like to offer you a two-year deal, Jim!

WHEN OLE GETS DESPERATE IN THE TRANSFER MARKET!

I'd love to go out for a meal, Ole!

An apple, banana and bread roll – all yours for £20!

WHEN CLIVE THE CAT CALLS KLOPP!

For the hundredth time – stop calling me, Clive!

EMOJI GAFFERS!

Can you guess which bossy-boots managers have hidden their faces?

1

My Blades are a sharp outfit!

2

I'm the Real deal!

3

I'm-a sticky, tricky toffee!

4

This'll catch you off guard!

5

This one's Gunner be tough!

6

I'll be frank, this is easy!

7

I'll be mad-rid if you don't get me!

One point for each correct answer!

TOTAL SCORE ☐ /7

THE 2📷 BEST PHOTOS OF MESSI!

Twenty years ago, a 13-year-old Lionel Messi moved to Barcelona with his family – to celebrate, we've picked our 20 fave pics of the greatest footballer of all time

1

ALL HAIL, KING LEO!

MAR 2017 Messi celebrates with the Barca fans at the Nou Camp after one of the greatest comebacks in UCL history – a 6-5 aggregate win over PSG!

PAZ SAYS
Messi has racked up an astonishing TEN La Liga titles during his time at Barcelona!

TURN OVER FOR MORE!

2 MEET THE FAM!

OCT 2003 Lionel poses with his mum, dad, sister, two brothers and his nephew back in his home town of Rosario, Argentina!

3 A REAL TALENT!

APR 2012 Not even three Real Madrid opponents – Pepe, Sergio Ramos and Fabio Coentrao – can stop Leo when he's in full flow in El Clasico!

4 OLYMPIC GOLD!

AUG 2008 Leo and his best mate Sergio Aguero celebrate winning the gold medal for Argentina at the Olympics in Bejiing, China!

6 PRICE OF GENIUS!

JUN 2015 Even the advertising hoardings know a thing or two about football these days – this was during Barcelona's 2015 UCL final clash with Juventus!

5 FIVE-MAN DEFENCE!

JUN 2010 South Korea stick five men on Messi during their 2010 World Cup clash – which Argentina win 4-1!

7 FOUR-SOME!

JUN 2015 Leo celebrates winning his fourth Champions League final after Barca beat Juve 3-1 at the Olympic Stadium in Berlin!

8 BEST OF ENEMIES!
OCT 2017 It's not often you see these two chatting – Cristiano Ronaldo and Leo catch up at the Best FIFA Football Awards ceremony in London!

9 THE PERFECT 10!
SEP 2017 The Catalan colours and Messi's famous No.10 shirt make this eye-catching photo – taken in Barca's 6-1 win v Eibar at the Nou Camp. Leo scored FOUR!

10 UP CLOSE WITH MESSI!
SEP 2019 Messi poses for a portrait ahead of The Best FIFA Football Awards 2019 at the Excelsior Hotel Gallia in Milan, Italy!

KETCH SAYS
Leo has won the Ballon d'Or award six times – one more than C-Ron!

11 JUMPING FOR JOY!
APR 2019 Celebration time for Leo as he bags two goals in Barcelona's 3-0 home win over Man. United in the UCL quarter-finals!

TURN OVER FOR MORE!

13 LETHAL LEO!

JUN 2014 He celebrates scoring a sick second-half winner against Bosnia & Herzegovina at the Maracana Stadium during the 2014 World Cup in Brazil!

12 RECORD BREAKER!

NOV 2014 Messi's Barcelona team-mates throw him into the air after he becomes La Liga's all-time record scorer following a goal against Sevilla at the Nou Camp!

15 THE HAND OF GOD!

MAY 2015 Messi, Suarez and Neymar – who became known as MSN and one of the game's most potent ever attacks – pose with the Copa Del Rey trophy!

14 DINKY DELIGHT!

MAY 2015 Just seconds after tying Bayern defender Jerome Boateng up in knots, Leo cheekily chips the ball past keeper Manuel Neuer during Barca's UCL semi-final win!

KETCH SAYS
Messi scored his first senior goal for Barca on 1 May 2005 against Albacete!

16 MAKE WAY FOR MESSI!

JUN 2016 Messi dribbles through a packed Chile defence in the 2016 Copa America final – in which Argentina lose on penalties!

17 THE REAL DEAL!

MAY 2018 Leo celebrates after scoring Barca's second goal in a 2-2 draw with Real Madrid at the Nou Camp!

19
THE WORLD'S BEST!
SEP 2019 Messi backstage at The Best FIFA Football Awards in Milan with his award for being the world's best player!

18
MAGICAL MESSI!
JUN 2018 Messi gloriously controls a 50-yard through-ball on his thigh before netting a huge goal for Argentina at the 2018 World Cup against Nigeria!

20
GOAL-DEN BOY!
DEC 2018 Leo poses with his FIVE European Golden Shoe awards – he then went on to win another one the following season!

PAZ SAYS
In the 2011-12 season, Leo smashed home 73 goals in 60 games – that's incredible!

IMMOBILE

MATCH of the DAY magazine

17

ITALY

MOTD MAG'S FOOTY LINGO!

Learn the beautiful game's very own language with Stobbsy

TOP BINS

Definition:
The area located in the top or bottom corners of the goal.

Example:
"Stick it in the top bins!"

CELE

Definition:
To rejoice using performative actions in expression of delight. Abbreviation of celebration.

Example:
"I don't know what was better – the goal or the cele after!"

JAX

Definition:
An action where one dummies the ball to confuse the opposition and regain possession.

Example:
"I'm behind you, jax it!"

WHIPPAGE

Definition:
Technique applied to the ball which causes it to move fast and suddenly in a specified direction.

Example:
"Woah. The whippage on that free-kick was unreal!"

ZING

Definition:
Hit with power and pinpoint precision, a pass that travels a long distance.

Example:
"Wow. She absolutely zinged that!"

PANNA

Definition:
The action in which a ball travels in between a player's legs due to the trickery of the baller in possession.

Example:
"Oh wow. That guy just got hit with a panna!"

WORLDIE

Definition:
A world-class attempt on goal which thunders into the back of the net in spectacular fashion.

Example:
"Vardy's hit that from 30 yards. What a worldie!"

SWAZ

Definition:
When one cuts across the ball to create a mid-flight, left-to-right twist through the air. Created by The F2.

Example:
"Bro, did you see the swaz on that pass?"

JOCKEY

Definition:
To shuffle using a side motion in front of an opponent – so a player doesn't get left on the ground with a tackle.

Example:
"Don't jump in – just jockey them!"

CARTOON

Get ready for epic LOLs with our fave MOTD mag throwback strips

Mo's calf woes!

Literally ridiculous!

Van Dijk's in hot water!

CLASSICS!

Illustrations: Paul Cemmick

Up to their old tricks!

Bruno to the rescue!

This is gonna age well!

THE A-Z

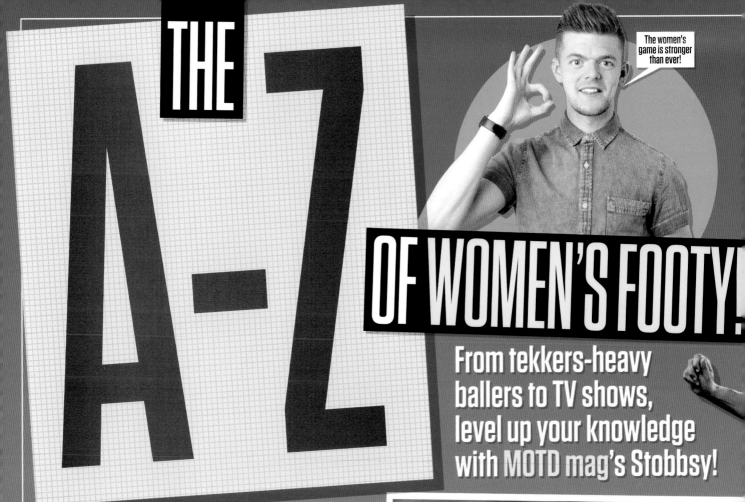

The women's game is stronger than ever!

OF WOMEN'S FOOTY!

From tekkers-heavy ballers to TV shows, level up your knowledge with **MOTD** mag's Stobbsy!

A IS FOR... Ada Hegerberg

Well, obvs. She's the best striker in the world, has scored more goals (144) than games played (117) for Lyon and is the first-ever winner of the Ballon d'Or Feminin award!

B IS FOR... Books

There are some really cool reads out there if you want to learn more or feel inspired by the women's game. Check out some of our faves below, including *Changing The Game* written by Man. United manager Casey Stoney. Class!

C IS FOR... Christine Sinclair

Canada's iconic baller has picked up 296 caps for her country – more than any other women's player. Consider this our big up for the 36-year-old!

E IS FOR... England national team

AKA The Lionesses! Lucy Bronze, Steph Houghton, Nikita Parris, Ellen White – and the list of tekky ballers goes on. We were hyped to get behind the squad during the 2019 World Cup and we can't wait for more big matches in the year ahead!

D IS FOR... Development

It's been so ledge to see women's football grow in stature over recent years and there's plenty more to come. From attendance increases to players and teams featuring on games like *FIFA*, we're moving in the right direction. Watch this space!

F IS FOR... FA CUP

The Women's FA Cup was founded in 1970 and goes from strength to strength every season with finals now held at Wembley. Arsenal are the bosses of this cup competition, with a record 14 trophy lifts!

Catch up with The Women's Football Show on BBC iPlayer

TURN OVER FOR MORE!

G IS FOR... GOAT

Mia must have to live in a mansion to store all the trophies she's bagged. From Olympic Golds to league titles, this all-action American hero is truly the greatest women's player of all time, with 158 goals in 276 games for the USA!

H IS FOR... History

There is so much to learn about the women's game. Did you know, for example, that the first ever women's footy match was North v South in 1895? Or that in 1920, a then-record 53,000 supporters watched Dick Kerr's Ladies v St. Helen's Ladies. Get studying all these amazing facts, readers!

I IS FOR... International footy

Everyone loves club football, but the international scene in the women's game is mad big. The summer tournaments attract huge crowds and help to grow the sport year after year. USA are currently the team to watch – they boss it!

J IS FOR...

Jamie Johnson

Who else loves watching *Jamie Johnson*? We're all over it, especially because there are so many incredible female players and role models to look up to in the show including Jack and Zoe. It's awesome to watch and learn from their journeys!

K IS FOR... Kelly Smith

If you don't know Kelly Smith, get to know. This legend of the game is England's all-time record goalscorer with 46 goals, has won five league titles and was awarded an MBE in the Queen's 2008 honour's list for her services to football!

L IS FOR... Lyon

Simply put, the French giants are the best team in the world! From league titles to the UWCL, they hoover up silverware every single season and have won 28 trophies in the past ten years alone. Their squad is unreal!

M IS FOR... Marta

Get this – Marta is the first player (male or female) to score at five World Cup tournaments. She also holds the women's record for goals scored at the competition with 17. The Brazil forward is regarded as one of the best players to ever play the game. Skills!

N IS FOR... New teams

With the women's game still growing all the time, new squads are popping up on the regs, which is brilliant to see. In 2018, Man. United reformed to be a part of the WSL, while Brighton and West Ham were founded at the start of the 1990s. Love it!

O IS FOR... Olympics

Women's football was added to the Olympic Games schedule in 1996 and we've never looked back. The summer tourneys are always a proper festival of footy, with Germany the current champions after winning the gold medal in 2016!

TURN OVER FOR MORE!

P IS FOR... Pundits

Some of the very best presenters and pundits in footy are women. Gabby Logan, Sue Smith, Eni Aluko and Alex Scott are just a few big names who put themselves in front of the camera and chat ball. Inspirational to see!

Q IS FOR... Quality boots

Everyone loves a limited edition pair and a long list of players have had some made to celebrate their epic individual successes in the women's game. From Alex Morgan's Phantoms to Megan Rapinoe's Mercurials, there are some straight-fire, heart-eyes versions out there right now!

R IS FOR... Record crowds

Season after season now, more people are engaging with women's football and attendance records continue to get smashed. The current highest turnout is 60,739, when Barcelona defeated Atletico Madrid at the Wanda Metropolitano Stadium in 2019!

T IS FOR... Tricks

Some of the sickest freestyle footballers on the planet are girls – Lisa Zimouche, Liv Cooke (pictured) and Charlotte Lade Rogers are three of the best in the game with a combined 2.8 million social media followers between them!

S IS FOR... She Believes Cup

In addition to all the other international competitions, every year we're treated to an amazing invitational women's tournament called the SheBelieves Cup. Held in the USA in late February or early March, this sick competition is contested by four teams and, you guessed it, the USA are the current champs!

U IS FOR... UEFA Euro 2021

Want something HUGE to look forward to? The next European Championships are being held in England from 6-31 July in 2022. It was meant to be played next year but the tourney was postponed for medical reasons. We can't wait for it!

UEFA WOMEN'S EURO 2021 ENGLAND

V IS FOR... Vivianne Miedema

Arsenal have always been the team to beat in English football, but when Holland striker Viv joined in 2017, she took them up another level. The current Women's Super League Player of the Year is, without doubt, the best player in English football!

W IS FOR... Women's Super League

Massive crunch matches, tense title races and boss-level ballers – established in 2010, the Women's Super League (WSL) is the highest league of women's football in England and it never disappoints. Chelsea are the current champions!

X IS FOR... X-Factor

There's nothing better than seeing flashes of star quality out on the pitch and the women's game is no different. Think Beth Mead's whipped finish against Everton, Sophie Ingle's cut volley against Arsenal or Lucy Bronze's first-time thwack against Norway. It's packed with wow moments!

Catch up with The Women's Football Show on BBC iPlayer BBC iPlayer

Y IS FOR... Youth

Hands up if you love a footy wonderkid? Snap! There are so many young players coming through and stepping up, including Man. City's Georgia Stanway, who is one of the most exciting talents in the game!

Z IS FOR... Zelem

Man. United midfielder Katie Zelem was named skipper of the club at the start of last season. The 24-year-old wears the No.10 shirt and is set to become a big name now she's playing for one of the world's most famous clubs. Katie scored seven in 21 WSL games last season and there's much more to come – watch this space!

MATCH of the **DAY** magazine

CAVANI

URUGUAY

RAMOS

SPAIN

MATCH of the **DAY**
magazine

THE STORY
THE STATS
THE SECRETS

Jadon
SANC

FACT FILE

FULL NAME: Jadon Malik Sancho **BORN:** London, England **DATE OF BIRTH:** 25 March 2000 (age 20) **HEIGHT:** 5ft 11in **POSITION:** Winger **FOOT:** Right

HO!

Three years ago, a 17-year-old English kid quit Man. City to join Borussia Dortmund. That kid is now the best young player on the planet. That kid is JADON SANCHO – and this is his story!

TURN OVER FOR MORE!

SANCHO'S STYLE!

Jadon has EVERYTHING an elite attacking player needs. He's super quick with amazing acceleration, he's got incredible close control, he can beat a man with pace or a trick, he's got mad vision to spot a pass and his finishing is 100 – serious tekkers!

FOOTY FOCUS Sancho has it all!

SANCHO'S STATS!

In three seasons with Dortmund, Jadon became the club's go-to star, their No.1 creative player and their match winner – the only young player in the world who compares to him is PSG megastar Kylian Mbappe. Just check out Jadon's sick numbers – this is A-list stuff!

CLUB CAREER			
SEASON	GAMES	GOALS	ASSISTS
2017-18	7 (5)	1	4
2018-19	26 (8)	12	14
2019-20*	25 (7)	17	16

INTERNATIONAL		
YEARS	TEAM	GAMES/GOALS
2015-16	England Under-16	11/7
2016-17	England Under-17	18/14
2017-18	England Under-19	7/2
2018-	England	11/2

*Stats correct up to 6 July 2020

SIMPLY THE CHEST His numbers are up there with Mbappe's!

SANCHO'S STORY!

● During the 2019-20 season, Jadon was directly involved in – by scoring or assisting – a Borussia Dortmund goal every 65 minutes. Elite-level tek!

● Jadon racked up more goals in the Bundesliga as a teenager than any other player in the league's history!

● Sancho is the first Englishman in 25 years to bag more than 15 goals AND 15 assists in a season in one of Europe's top footy leagues!

CHAMP Jadon with the German Supercup trophy!

A LEGEND IN THE MAKING!

Sancho nets his first England goal v Kosovo in a 5-3 win in September 2019!

It's crazy but it's true – Jadon's numbers are BETTER than Lionel Messi's AND Cristiano Ronaldo's at the same age

MESSI
70
GAMES
26
GOALS
8
ASSISTS

SANCHO
90
GAMES
31
GOALS
42
ASSISTS

RONALDO
107
GAMES
16
GOALS
16
ASSISTS

*Stats when all players turned 20 years old

"Playing for England is something I'll never forget!"
... Sancho

KETCH SAYS
Sancho took a big gamble by moving to Germany at such a young age – but it's proved a masterstroke!

Listen to live England games on BBC Radio 5 live

LONDON
25 MARCH 2000
Born in Camberwell, south London

2007
Joins Watford's academy aged seven

MARCH 2015
Moves to Man. City for an initial £66,000

MAY 2017
Helps England Under-17s to the final of the Euros

AUGUST 2017
Joins Borussia Dortmund for £8 million

OCTOBER 2017
Part of the England squad that wins the Under-17 World Cup

TURN OVER FOR PART 2

7 THINGS YOU NEED TO KNOW ABOUT SANCHO!

Sancho finished third in the UEFA Nations League with England in 2018-19!

PAZ SAYS
Jadon played in the England team that finished runners-up at the 2017 Euro Under-17 Championship!

STYLISH Jadon's strong look!

1 SANCH'S SICK STYLE!

He brings the sauce on the grass and he's got it locked off the pitch, too. Whether he's on the red carpet or on his way to training, the boy Jadon always looks on point!

2 LEAVING HOME!

When he was just 12 years old, Jadon left home to board at Watford's epic academy. Even at that age he was determined to become one of the best players in the world one day!

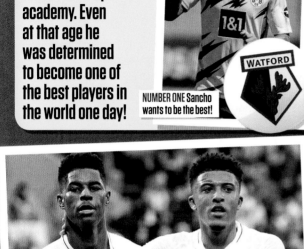
NUMBER ONE Sancho wants to be the best!

PALS Cal-Huds and Sanch!

3 LONDON MATES

Jadon is huge mates with Chelsea star Callum Hudson-Odoi and Arsenal youngster Reiss Nelson. He played youth footy with Nelson!

RATED Rash loves Jadon's tek!

4 MAD LOVE FOR SANCHO!

Man. United star Marcus Rashford is a fan. "He plays off the cuff, he's creative and imaginative – you need this to be world class," Rash says!

> ## "He plays off the cuff, he's creative and imaginative!"
> Marcus Rashford

BIG DEAL City offered Jadon a mega deal to try to keep him!

5 JADON'S PEP TALK!

Man. City were desperate to keep Jadon at the club, but he decided he had a better chance of first-team football at Dortmund!

6 HIS IDOL WAS RONALDINHO!

Jadon wanted to be Brazil legend Ronaldinho as a kid – his mates say he used to watch clips of him when teachers weren't looking!

7 BLUE WAS THE COLOUR!

As a kid growing up in London, Jadon supported Chelsea. His favourite players at the time were current boss Frank Lampard and ex-goal machine Didier Drogba!

BLUE ARE YA? Sancho adored Drog and Lamps!

OCTOBER 2018
Makes his England debut v Croatia in the Nations League

OCTOBER 2018
Is named Bundesliga Player of the Month

MAY 2019
Is named in Bundesliga Team of the Year for 2018-19 season

AUGUST 2019
Helps Dortmund to a 2-0 German Super Cup win over Bayern Munich

SEPTEMBER 2019
Scores first senior England goals when he nets twice v Kosovo in a Euro 2020 qualifier

MAY 2020
Scores the first hat-trick of his career when he hits three against Paderborn

SADIO **MANE**

SENEGAL

ENGLAND

KANE

WHO'S YOUR FAVOURITE KING?

I'm the king!

Thou ist mistaken, bro!

JOSH KING or KING HENRY VIII?

It's the question the whole world has NOT been asking – but join our ding-dong debate!

JOSH KING		KING HENRY VIII
Joshua Christian Kojo King	**FULL NAME**	Henry Tudor
Born in Oslo, the capital of Norway, in 1992 – he's 28 years old	**BORN**	Born in London, capital of England, in 1491 – that's 529 years ago
Quick Norwegian forward who's a ruthless goalscorer	**WHO IS HE?**	Portly English monarch who was a ruthless, hot-tempered bully
Feasting on juicy through-balls played by Steve Cook	**YOU'LL SEE HIM...**	Feasting on juicy chicken legs roasted by his cook
Having played for six clubs and being The Cherries' top scorer in 2017	**WHAT'S HE FAMOUS FOR?**	Having six wives and being England's top ruler in the 1500s
Scored against Burnley's Nick Pope in 2018, securing a great result at Turf Moor	**WHAT'S THAT ABOUT THE POPE?**	Ditched the Pope and Catholic Church in 1533, declaring himself the head of a new Church Of England
Not known for his heading – just one of his 46 Premier League goals has been with his bonce	**HEADING**	Known more for beheading than heading. He beheaded more wives (two) than Josh King has scored headers

STEVE COOK

A COOK

NICK POPE

THE POPE

JOSH IS MY FAVOURITE KING ☑ ☑ **HENRY VIII IS MY FAVOURITE KING**

OTHER KINGS AVAILABLE!

KING CHARLES SPANIEL

KING KONG

KING EDWARD POTATO

KING-SIZE BED

BREAKFAST 6AM
BURGER KING

LEGENDS DREAM TEAM!

MOTD mag brings you an all-star 11 of the best ballers to ever play the beautiful game. Check it!

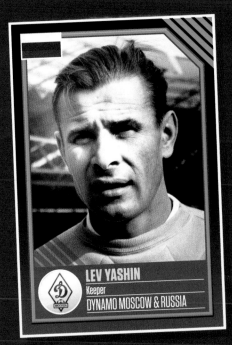

LEV YASHIN
Keeper
DYNAMO MOSCOW & RUSSIA

CAFU
Right-back
AC MILAN & BRAZIL

FRANCO BARESI
Centre-back
AC MILAN & ITALY

FRANZ BECKENBAUER
Centre-back
BAYERN MUNICH & GERMANY

PAOLO MALDINI
Left-back
AC MILAN & ITALY

Formation

YASHIN
CAFU BECKENBAUER BARESI MALDINI
MATTHAUS
ZIDANE XAVI
MESSI PELE RONALDO

LOTHAR MATTHAUS
Defensive midfielder
BAYERN MUNICH & GERMANY

ZINEDINE ZIDANE
Midfielder
REAL MADRID & FRANCE

XAVI
Midfielder
BARCELONA & SPAIN

LIONEL MESSI
Right forward
BARCELONA & ARGENTINA

CRISTIANO RONALDO
Left forward
JUVENTUS & PORTUGAL

PELE
Striker
SANTOS & BRAZIL

PICK YOUR POSITION!

Been scratching your head wondering where to play on the pitch? Don't worry – we've got you covered!

THE ROLE MODEL
GIANLUIGI BUFFON
Gigi once went 974 minutes without conceding a goal – a footy world record!

KEEPER!

POSTION: Saving shots, diving into the top corner and keeping the ball from hitting the back of the net isn't the only job of a keeper. Your distribution needs to be on point, you need to be open to receiving a pass and also super organised to help position the defence!

THE KEY ATTRIBUTES

 REFLEXES

 FOCUS

 POSITIONING

MY NEW POSITION:

RIGHT-BACK!

POSTION: Stationed to the right of the centre-backs, you'll provide protection from oppo wingers. The key is to stop crosses, prevent moves into the box and cover fellow defenders. Must also support attacking play with runs, crosses and pattern of play passes!

THE KEY ATTRIBUTES

  RIGHT-FOOTED

 STAMINA

 TACKLING

MY NEW POSITION: ✔

THE ROLE MODEL DANI ALVES
The Brazil defender is the most decorated player of all time with 41 trophy wins!

LEFT-BACK!

POSTION: The role of a left-back is identical to RB – just on the opposite side. Right-sided wingers will try to cut into the box or get around you to whip one in, but your aim is to stop these things with interceptions, blocks and tackles. Top full-backs get forward, too!

THE KEY ATTRIBUTES

 LEFT-FOOTED

 STAMINA

 TACKLING

MY NEW POSITION: ✔

THE ROLE MODEL ANDY ROBERTSON
Robbo has gone from Championship footy with Hull to winning UCL and Prem titles in just three years!

Keep up to date with the latest done deals at bbc.co.uk/sport/football/transfers BBC SPORT

TURN OVER FOR MORE!

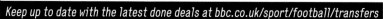

SWEEPER!

POSTION: A sweeping centre-back plays slightly behind the defence to add extra security and, well, sweep up the ball if a player gets through the defensive line. You're not expected to man-mark, must read the game well and be able to create phases of ball from deep!

THE KEY ATTRIBUTES

ANTICIPATION   REACTIONS   PACE

MY NEW POSITION:

CENTRE -BACK!

POSTION: There are many types of traditional CBs – stoppers, ball-players, man-markers – but the job is largely the same: keep strikers quiet and defend the goal at all costs. You must be a committed tackler, strong in the air and focused with your positioning. Be alert!

THE KEY ATTRIBUTES

TACKLING   HEADING   FOCUS

MY NEW POSITION:

DEFENSIVE MIDFIELDER!

POSTION: A team's DM must be disciplined to hold their position of protection between defence and midfield. You'll break up any advancing attacks with interceptions and tackles, pressure the opposition in possession and also start attacking phases from deep!

THE KEY ATTRIBUTES

 ANTICIPATION

 TACKLING

 STRENGTH

MY NEW POSITION: ✓

THE ROLE MODEL N'GOLO KANTE
Chelsea's defensive destroyer has won two Prem titles, a World Cup and the PFA Players' POTY award!

THE ROLE MODEL LUKA MODRIC
Luka ended Messi and Ronaldo's run of winning every Ballon D'or since 2007!

CENTRAL MIDFIELDER!

POSTION: A midfield maestro must pull the strings of play with pinpoint passes, charge around the pitch from box to box and break up opposition possession with perfectly timed challenges. You are probably the most important cog in any elite starting 11 machine!

THE KEY ATTRIBUTES

 STAMINA

 PASSING

 VISION

MY NEW POSITION: ✓

TURN OVER FOR MORE! ➤

ATTACKING MIDFIELDER!

POSTION: An attacking mid, or CAM, is positioned in an advanced central position and expected to knit together attacking moves with through-balls, positive dribbles and runs into space. You're also expected to contribute to goalscoring, so pop off your shots from range!

THE KEY ATTRIBUTES

 DRIBBLING

 CREATIVITY

 FINISHING

MY NEW POSITION: ✔

THE ROLE MODEL KEVIN DE BRUYNE
KDB has bagged more than 60 assists and 30 goals since he started playing in the Prem!

THE ROLE MODEL DAVID BECKHAM
This Man. United and England ledge picked up 80 assists in the Prem during his career!

RIGHT WING!

POSTION: A traditional winger is expected to get past their opponent and deliver pinpoint crosses to their strikers. But unlike in the full-back position, a wide forward can be left or right footed – if you can also cut inside and shoot, you'll be a real threat for your team!

THE KEY ATTRIBUTES

 PACE

 CREATIVITY

 CROSSING

MY NEW POSITION:

LEFT WING!

LW

POSTION: In the modern game, wide forwards are often strong with their opposite foot, too. This means the left-sided player can cut inside and get shots off with their right. Their key role is to use skill to link with the striker to create chances, score goals and bag assists!

THE KEY ATTRIBUTES

 PACE

 CREATIVITY

 CROSSING

MY NEW POSITION: ✔

THE ROLE MODEL KYLIAN MBAPPE
At just 19 years old, Kylian Mbappe won Best Young Player at the 2018 World Cup with France!

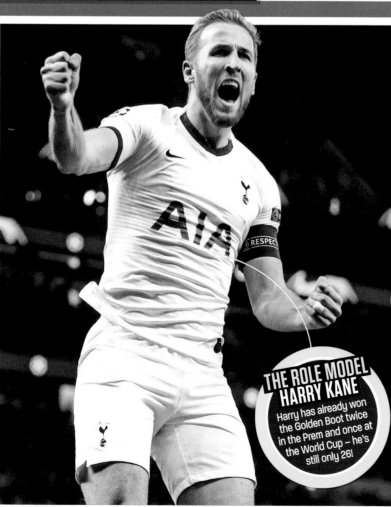

THE ROLE MODEL HARRY KANE
Harry has already won the Golden Boot twice in the Prem and once at the World Cup – he's still only 26!

STRIKER!

ST

POSTION: In the modern game, wide forwards can be more dangerous moving inside on their stronger foot – so a left-sided player can fire off shots with their right. Your key role is to use your silky skills to link up with your striker to create chances, score goals and bag assists!

THE KEY ATTRIBUTES

 STRENGTH

 FINISHING

 COMPOSURE

MY NEW POSITION: ✔

Check out the latest transfer rumours at bbc.co.uk/sport/football/gossip gossip

POLAND

LEWANDOWSKI

THROWBACK SNAPS!

Your fave ballers haven't always looked as cool as they do now

FIFA FLAS

VIRGIL VAN DIJK

	FIFA 16	FIFA 17	FIFA 18	FIFA 19	FIFA 20
Rating	77 CB	79 CB	83 CB	85 CB	90 CB
	VAN DIJK	VAN DIJK	VAN DIJK	VAN DIJK	VAN DIJK

FIFA 16 — 67 PAC / 67 DRI / 60 SHO / 77 DEF / 64 PAS / 83 PHY

FIFA 17 — 67 PAC / 67 DRI / 61 SHO / 79 DEF / 65 PAS / 83 PHY

FIFA 18 — 2★ Skills / 3★ W. Foot / H/M — 73 PAC / 70 DRI / 60 SHO / 83 DEF / 67 PAS / 85 PHY

FIFA 19 — 71 PAC / 70 DRI / 60 SHO / 85 DEF / 67 PAS / 84 PHY

FIFA 20 — 77 PAC / 72 DRI / 60 SHO / 90 DEF / 70 PAS / 86 PHY

SERGE GNABRY

	FIFA 16	FIFA 17	FIFA 18	FIFA 19	FIFA 20
Rating	70 RM	77 LM	79 LM	82 LM	84 RM
	GNABRY	GNABRY	GNABRY	GNABRY	GNABRY

  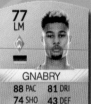  

FIFA 16 — 84 PAC / 75 DRI / 60 SHO / 43 DEF / 65 PAS / 63 PHY

FIFA 17 — 88 PAC / 81 DRI / 74 SHO / 43 DEF / 69 PAS / 66 PHY

FIFA 18 — 4★ Skills / 3★ W. Foot / H/M — 90 PAC / 82 DRI / 76 SHO / 43 DEF / 71 PAS / 67 PHY

FIFA 19 — 91 PAC / 85 DRI / 81 SHO / 44 DEF / 72 PAS / 67 PHY

FIFA 20 — 90 PAC / 85 DRI / 82 SHO / 43 DEF / 75 PAS / 69 PHY

HARRY MAGUIRE

	FIFA 16	FIFA 17	FIFA 18	FIFA 19	FIFA 20
Rating	69 CB	72 CB	75 CB	82 CB	82 CB
	MAGUIRE	MAGUIRE	MAGUIRE	MAGUIRE	MAGUIRE

FIFA 16 — 46 PAC / 43 DRI / 35 SHO / 70 DEF / 53 PAS / 78 PHY

FIFA 17 — 47 PAC / 51 DRI / 35 SHO / 71 DEF / 53 PAS / 80 PHY

FIFA 18 — 2★ Skills / 3★ W. Foot / M/M — 44 PAC / 60 DRI / 37 SHO / 75 DEF / 56 PAS / 82 PHY

FIFA 19 — 47 PAC / 69 DRI / 46 SHO / 81 DEF / 63 PAS / 82 PHY

FIFA 20 — 50 PAC / 70 DRI / 53 SHO / 81 DEF / 64 PAS / 84 PHY

JAMES MADDISON

	FIFA 16	FIFA 17	FIFA 18	FIFA 19	FIFA 20
Rating	64 CF	68 CAM	74 CAM	75 CAM	82 CAM
	MADDISON	MADDISON	MADDISON	MADDISON	MADDISON

 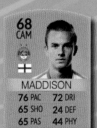  

FIFA 16 — 77 PAC / 67 DRI / 64 SHO / 24 DEF / 62 PAS / 44 PHY

FIFA 17 — 76 PAC / 72 DRI / 65 SHO / 24 DEF / 65 PAS / 44 PHY

FIFA 18 — 3★ Skills / 4★ W. Foot / H/M — 76 PAC / 75 DRI / 70 SHO / 31 DEF / 73 PAS / 50 PHY

FIFA 19 — 74 PAC / 76 DRI / 73 SHO / 39 DEF / 75 PAS / 48 PHY

FIFA 20 — 76 PAC / 82 DRI / 77 SHO / 39 DEF / 84 PAS / 57 PHY

HBACK!

These ballers have had a FUT shield glow-up over the years!

BERNARDO SILVA

	FIFA 16	FIFA 17	FIFA 18	FIFA 19	FIFA 20
Rating	79 RM	81 RM	84 RM	84 RW	87 RW
Name	BERNARDO SILVA	BERNARDO SILVA	SILVA	BERNARDO SILVA	SILVA
PAC	79	79	81	78	81
SHO	68	69	72	72	76
PAS	77	78	81	83	83
DRI	82	83	89	89	92
DEF	45	45	45	46	51
PHY	60	60	61	58	67

FIFA 18 — 4★ Skills, 3★ W. Foot, M/M

ADAMA TRAORE

 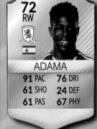 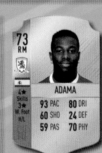  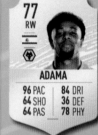

	FIFA 16	FIFA 17	FIFA 18	FIFA 19	FIFA 20
Rating	71 RW	72 RW	73 RM	75 RW	77 RW
Name	ADAMA	ADAMA	ADAMA	ADAMA	ADAMA
PAC	90	91	93	96	96
SHO	61	61	60	61	64
PAS	60	61	59	64	64
DRI	74	76	80	83	84
DEF	24	24	24	25	36
PHY	68	67	70	75	78

FIFA 18 — 4★ Skills, 3★ W. Foot, H/L

FRENKIE DE JONG

	FIFA 16	FIFA 17	FIFA 18	FIFA 19	FIFA 20
Rating	63 CM	66 CM	75 CM	77 CM	85 CM
Name	DE JONG	DE JONG	DE JONG	DE JONG	DE JONG
PAC	66	62	76	73	79
SHO	51	51	56	56	64
PAS	65	67	78	79	84
DRI	65	70	83	84	88
DEF	48	47	60	66	76
PHY	52	51	65	65	76

FIFA 18 — 3★ Skills, 3★ W. Foot, H/M

TIMO WERNER

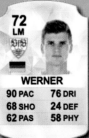 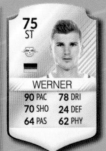   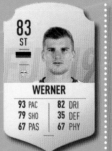

	FIFA 16	FIFA 17	FIFA 18	FIFA 19	FIFA 20
Rating	72 LM	75 ST	82 ST	83 ST	86 ST
Name	WERNER	WERNER	WERNER	WERNER	WERNER
PAC	90	90	91	93	92
SHO	68	70	79	79	84
PAS	62	64	65	67	71
DRI	76	78	80	82	84
DEF	24	24	28	35	36
PHY	58	62	65	67	71

FIFA 18 — 3★ Skills, 4★ W. Foot, H/M

CROATIA

MODRIC

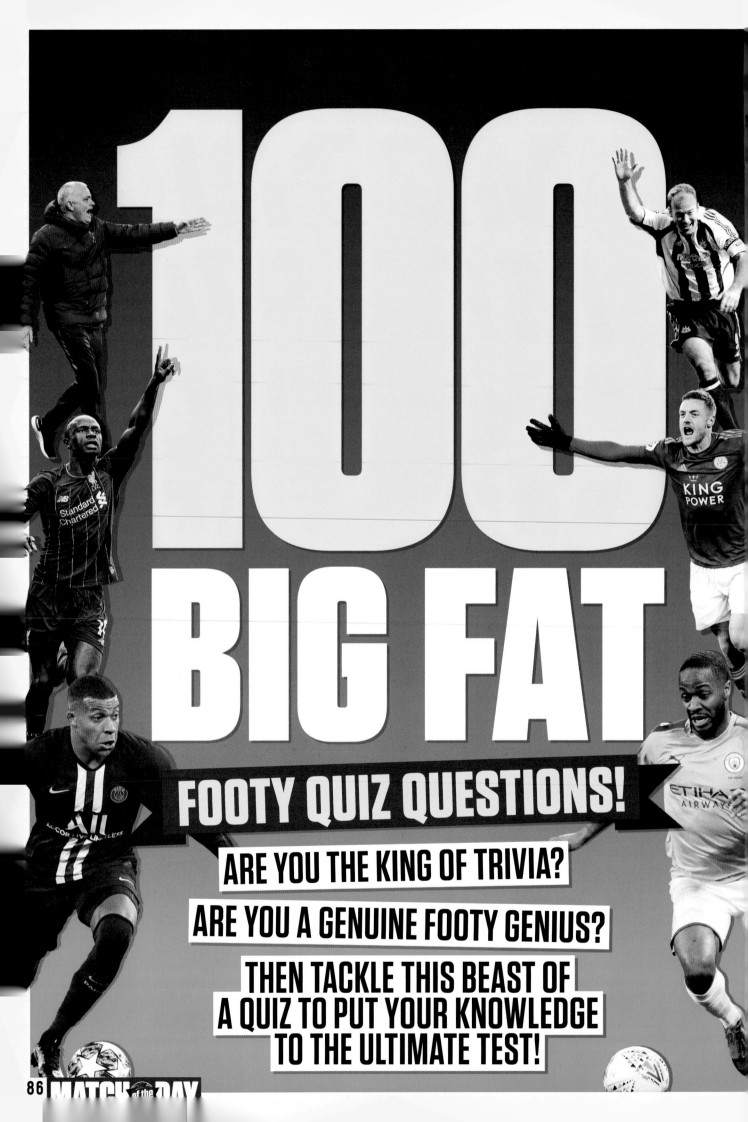

100 BIG FAT

FOOTY QUIZ QUESTIONS!

ARE YOU THE KING OF TRIVIA?

ARE YOU A GENUINE FOOTY GENIUS?

THEN TACKLE THIS BEAST OF A QUIZ TO PUT YOUR KNOWLEDGE TO THE ULTIMATE TEST!

PREMIER LEAGUE!

HOW MUCH DO YOU KNOW ABOUT THE WORLD'S NO.1 LEAGUE?

TITLE WINNERS! Put these legends in order of how many Prem titles they've won. One = most titles, five = fewest titles!

1 AGUERO	2 SHEARER	3 LAMPARD	4 FABREGAS	5 ROONEY

6 GUESS WHO! Who is this current Prem striker pictured five years ago?

ANSWER

7 CAREER PATH! Name this Prem star from his footy career!

QUEEN'S PARK
2012-13

DUNDEE UNITED
2013-14

HULL
2014-17

LIVERPOOL
2017-PRESENT

ANSWER

8 PORTO PUZZLER! Which current Prem boss signed Wolves gaffer Nuno Espirito Santo as a player for Porto in 2002?

ANSWER

 **THE LIFE OF RAHEEM?** Are these statements about the Man. City and England ace true or false?

12 He was born in Croydon, south London

ANSWER

13 He joined Liverpool from MK Dons

ANSWER

14 His middle name is Shaquille

ANSWER

15 He has won the Premier League twice

ANSWER

GOALS GALORE! Are these superstar strikers the record Premier League goalscorers for their clubs – yes or no?

9 JAMIE VARDY Leicester

Yes ☐
No ☐

10 CHRIS WOOD Burnley
Yes ☐
No ☐

11 DIDIER DROGBA Chelsea

Yes ☐
No ☐

ROUND 2 FOOTBALL LEAGUE!

NAME EACH EFL CLUB BELOW FROM THE BADGE AND THE STADIUM NAME

16

Stadium: Deepdale

ANSWER

17

Stadium: Hillsborough

ANSWER

18

Stadium: KCOM Stadium

ANSWER

19

Stadium: Liberty Stadium

ANSWER

20

Stadium: Ewood Park

ANSWER

21

Stadium: Adams Park

ANSWER

22

Stadium: Priestfield Stadium

ANSWER

23

Stadium: Bloomfield Road

ANSWER

24

Stadium: Stadium Of Light

ANSWER

25

Stadium: County Ground

ANSWER

26

Stadium: Glanford Park

ANSWER

27

Stadium: Blundell Park

ANSWER

28

Stadium: Kenilworth Road

ANSWER

29

Stadium: Riverside Stadium

ANSWER

30

Stadium: Memorial Stadium

ANSWER

31 FRENCH PHENOMENON! PSG signed Kylian Mbappe from which Ligue 1 rival in 2017?

ANSWER

32 KINGS OF SPAIN! Which club has won La Liga the most times in the league's history?

ANSWER

33 COUNTRY CLASH! If you were watching Willem II v Twente which country would you be in?

ANSWER

34 GERMAN GIANT! Which awesome club has the biggest stadium in the Bundesliga?

ANSWER

35 JUVE GOT TO BE JOKING! The last time Juve didn't win Serie A was 2010-11 – who won it that season?

ANSWER

36 BARCA SLOGAN! What does Barcelona's motto Mes Que Un Club mean in English?

ANSWER

37 EUROTEASER! Which country do clubs like Malmo, AIK and IFK Norrkoping come from?

ANSWER

CHAMPIONS LEAGUE CHAMPIONS! Have these elite European clubs ever won a UCL trophy – yes or no?

38
Yes No

39
Yes No

40
Yes No

41
Yes No

42
Yes No

43
Yes No

44
Yes No

45
Yes No

REAL OR FAKE GAFFERS? Have these bosses ever been manager of Real Madrid – yes or no?

46 RANIERI
Yes No

47 ANCELOTTI
Yes No

48 PELLEGRINI
Yes No

49 MOURINHO
Yes No

50 BENITEZ
Yes No

ROUND 4 RAPID FIRE QUESTIONS!

TEST YOUR GENERAL KNOWLEDGE IN OUR 60-SECOND CHALLENGE

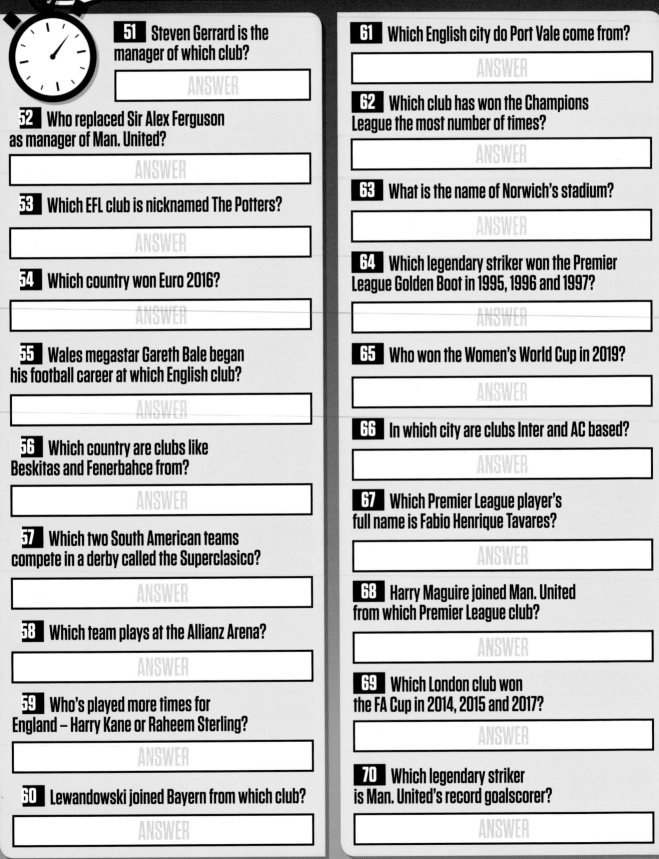

51 Steven Gerrard is the manager of which club?

ANSWER

52 Who replaced Sir Alex Ferguson as manager of Man. United?

ANSWER

53 Which EFL club is nicknamed The Potters?

ANSWER

54 Which country won Euro 2016?

ANSWER

55 Wales megastar Gareth Bale began his football career at which English club?

ANSWER

56 Which country are clubs like Beskitas and Fenerbahce from?

ANSWER

57 Which two South American teams compete in a derby called the Superclasico?

ANSWER

58 Which team plays at the Allianz Arena?

ANSWER

59 Who's played more times for England – Harry Kane or Raheem Sterling?

ANSWER

60 Lewandowski joined Bayern from which club?

ANSWER

61 Which English city do Port Vale come from?

ANSWER

62 Which club has won the Champions League the most number of times?

ANSWER

63 What is the name of Norwich's stadium?

ANSWER

64 Which legendary striker won the Premier League Golden Boot in 1995, 1996 and 1997?

ANSWER

65 Who won the Women's World Cup in 2019?

ANSWER

66 In which city are clubs Inter and AC based?

ANSWER

67 Which Premier League player's full name is Fabio Henrique Tavares?

ANSWER

68 Harry Maguire joined Man. United from which Premier League club?

ANSWER

69 Which London club won the FA Cup in 2014, 2015 and 2017?

ANSWER

70 Which legendary striker is Man. United's record goalscorer?

ANSWER

INTERNATIONAL ICONS!

WHICH COUNTRIES DO THESE BRILLIANT BALLERS PLAY FOR?

71 LUIS SUAREZ

ANSWER

72 THIAGO ALCANTARA

ANSWER

73 NABIL FEKIR

ANSWER

74 MARIO MANDZUKIC

ANSWER

75 DOUGLAS COSTA

ANSWER

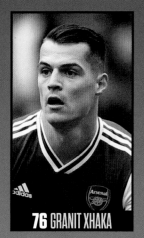

76 GRANIT XHAKA

ANSWER

77 ILKAY GUNDOGAN

ANSWER

78 HEUNG-MIN SON

ANSWER

79 VICTOR LINDELOF

ANSWER

80 AXEL WITSEL

ANSWER

81 JUAN CUADRADO

ANSWER

82 SADIO MANE

ANSWER

83 ARTURO VIDAL

ANSWER

84 CIRO IMMOBILE

ANSWER

85 HIRVING LOZANO

ANSWER

ROUND 6 RETRO FOOTY!

YOU MIGHT NEED TO GRAB YOUR MUM OR DAD FOR HELP WITH THESE

86 KING JOHAN! Which country did playmaker Johan Cruyff play for?

`ANSWER`

87 PREM LEDGEND! Italian baller Ginafranco Zola played for which Prem club?

`ANSWER`

88 WORLD CUP WINNERS! Which team is this lining up at the 1990 World Cup?

`ANSWER`

89 KOP IDOL! Who has played the most Premier League games for Liverpool?

`ANSWER`

90 BIG MONEY BECKS! David Beckham left Man. United in 2003 to join which club?

`ANSWER`

91 THE THREE LIONS LEADER! Who was manager of the famous England team at Euro 96?

`ANSWER`

OLD SCHOOL HEROES! Can you name these Premier League stars of yesteryear?

92 GOAL-DEN BOY! He was a two-time winner of the Premier League Golden Boot!

`ANSWER`

93 SHOWBOATING STAR! A hero at Bolton between 2002 and 2006 – this guy was a true entertainer!

`ANSWER`

94 DEFENSIVE ROCK! This no-nonsense centre-back was a title winner back in 1995!

`ANSWER`

95 MR GOALS! This powerful frontman played for SIX different Premier League clubs!

`ANSWER`

ROUND 7

WOMEN'S FOOTY!

CAN YOU NAME THESE ICONS OF THE WOMEN'S GAME?

96

ANSWER

97

ANSWER

98

ANSWER

99

ANSWER

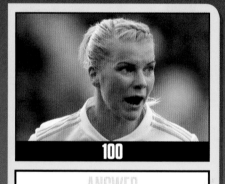

100

ANSWER

QUIZ ANSWERS

ROUND 1 PREMIER LEAGUE!
36 More than a club
37 Sweden
38 No
39 Yes
40 No
41 No
42 Yes
43 Yes
44 Yes
45 No
46 No
47 No
48 Yes
49 Yes
50 Yes
51 Rangers
52 David Moyes
53 Stoke
54 Portugal
55 Southampton
56 Turkey
57 Boca Juniors and River Plate
58 Bayern Munich
59 Raheem Sterling
60 B. Dortmund
61 Stoke-on-Trent
62 Real Madrid
63 Carrow Road
64 Alan Shearer
65 USA
66 Milan

ROUND 2 RAPID-FIRE Q'S
1 2 2 5 3 3 4 4 5 1

ROUND 3 EUROPEAN FOOTY
67 Fabinho
68 Leicester
69 Arsenal
70 Wayne Rooney

ROUND 4 FOOTBALL LEAGUE!
17 Sheff. Wed.
16 Preston
18 Hull
19 Swansea
20 Blackburn
21 Wycombe
22 Gillingham
23 Blackpool
24 Sunderland
25 Swindon
26 Scunthorpe
27 Grimsby
28 Luton
29 Middlesbrough
30 Bristol Rovers
31 Monaco
32 Real Madrid
33 Holland
34 B. Dortmund
35 AC Milan

ROUND 5 INTERNATIONAL ICONS!
100 Ada Hegerberg
99 Lucy Bronze
98 Vivianne Miedema
97 Sam Kerr
96 Megan Rapinoe

WOMEN'S FOOTY! ROUND 7
95 Les Ferdinand
94 Colin Hendry
93 Jay-Jay Okocha
92 Jimmy Floyd Hasselbaink
91 Terry Venables
90 Real Madrid
89 Jamie Carragher
88 West Germany
87 Chelsea
86 Holland
RETRO FOOTY!
85 Mexico
84 Italy
83 Chile
82 Senegal
81 Colombia
80 Belgium
79 Sweden
78 South Korea
77 Germany
76 Switzerland
75 Brazil
74 Croatia
73 France
72 Spain
71 Uruguay

ROUND 6

FINAL SCORE!

0-25
EFL CUP
Not the greatest total score ever, but it still counts as silverware!

26-50
FA CUP
Nice – a trophy in the cabinet. Keep at it and you can achieve more!

51-75
PREMIER LEAGUE
Great work. With more work at training, you'll reach the top!

76-100
CHAMPIONS LEAGUE
BOOM – you've totally crushed it. We're so impressed!

SALAH

EGYPT

MATCH of the **DAY** magazine